Donated to:

St. Mary's

by

Father Bill Feldner, S.V.D

date:

May 11, 1992

Who Made These Things?

Joyce Wood Crapps • Illustrated by Mike Sloan

Broadman Press
Nashville, Tennessee

#2564

© Copyright 1987 • Broadman Press
All rights reserved.
4241-78

ISBN: 0-8054-4178-6
Library of Congress Catalog Card Number: 86-18773
Dewey Decimal Classification: C231
Subject Heading: GOD

Printed in the United States of America

Library of Congress Cataloging-in-Publication Data

Crapps, Joyce Wood, 1945-
  Who made these things?

  (Bible-and-me)
  Summary: Explains that God created the earth, sky,
plants, animals, and people, and that people need to
thank God for his love and care.
  1. Creation—Juvenile literature.   2. Providence and
government of God—Juvenile literature.   3. God—
Love—Juvenile literature.   [1. Creation.   2. God]
I. Sloan, Mike, ill.   II. Title.   III. Series.
BT695.C67   1987   231.7'65   86-18773
ISBN 0-8054-4178-6

To
My husband, Richard,
and
My children, Hank and Elizabeth

We can take a nature walk outside.

What will we see?

Up in the blue sky are white clouds and a bright sun.

In the nighttime sky we see stars and a
moon.

Who made these things?

God did! He made the sky, clouds, and
sun. God made the stars and moon.

"Swirl, swirl," goes the water around the rocks in the stream. The water is cool. The rocks are hard.

"Thump, thump," go our feet on the dirt.
We can dig in the dirt.

Look! Now it's raining. Our dirt turns to
mud. "Splat, splat," I like to feel the mud.

Who made these things?
God did! He made the cool water and
hard rocks. God made the dirt and rain.

It's fun to visit the seashore. The ocean's waves roll over the sand. The sand tickles our feet as the waves roll over them.

See the pretty seashells. A little sea animal
once lived in the seashell. We can put the
shells in our bucket and take them home.

Come quick and look! A crab ran across
the sand. He made a hole in the sand. The
seashore is his home.

Who made these things?
God did! He made the ocean's waves and seashells. God made the crab and seashore.

"Woo, woo," blows the wind through the tall trees. The leaves are green. Yellow dandelions are growing by the trees.

Let's sit under the tree and look around.
What do we see! We see green grass and
wild flowers. We see tall mountains.

Look! There is an apple tree with big red apples.

Who made these things?

God did! He made the tall trees and short trees. God made trees that grow fruit. He made the apple trees. He made the dandelions and wild flowers. God made the mountains tall and beautiful.

Let's walk through Grandpa's garden.

Grandpa said, "God made our world. He made good food for us to eat. God made vegetables to grow on plants and vines."

Here is the food we found in Grandpa's garden.

Who made these things?
God did! God made our food.

"Swish, swish," swim the fish. Big fish and little fish live in oceans and rivers.

Who made these fish? God did! He made the big fish and little fish.

"Peck, peck, peck." Listen. High in a tree are two woodpeckers.

Who made these birds? God did! God made the woodpeckers and all the other birds flying high in the sky.

"Moo, moo," says the brown cow. The
cow walks slowly over to the fresh hay.

"Chitter, chatter," says the squirrel. Up a tree he runs. He stops and looks up.

Who made these things? God did! God made the cow. God made the squirrel. God made all the animals.

Many people live in our world. Some people are tall and some are short. Some people have black hair and some people have blond hair.

Who made these people?
God did! He made mothers and daddies.
He made boys and girls.

Our family likes to sing, "La, la, God loves me."

God made grandmamas and grandpapas.

God made mothers and daddies.

God made brothers and sisters.

God made little babies.

God is good to us. He gave us many
things to enjoy. Thank You, God, for making
all these things.